A Young Citizen's Guide to News Literacy

# CONSPIRACY THEORIES AND FAKE NEWS

## Phil Corso

**PowerKIDS**
press™

New York

Published in 2019 by The Rosen Publishing Group, Inc.
29 East 21st Street, New York, NY 10010

First Edition

Editor: Jill Keppeler
Book Design: Reann Nye

Photo Credits: Cover vitranc/E+/Getty Images; p. 5 John Lamb/ DigitalVision/Getty Images; p. 7 Buncha Lim/Shutterstock.com; p. 9 Larry Busacca/ Getty Images Entertainment/Getty Images; p. 11 Courtesy of NASA; p. 13 Georgejmclittle/Shutterstock.com; p. 15 Bettmann/Getty Images; p. 17 AFP/Getty Images; p. 19 The Washington Post/Getty Images; p. 21 Twin Design/Shutterstock.com; p. 23 dennizn/ Shutterstock.com; p. 25 Rawpixel.com/Shutterstock.com; p. 27 johnnyscriv/E+/Getty Images; p. 29 Lawrey/Shutterstock.com; p. 30 GaudiLab/Shutterstock.com.

Library of Congress Cataloging-in-Publication Data

Names: Corso, Phil.
Title: Conspiracy theories and fake news / Phil Corso.
Description: New York : PowerKids Press, 2019. | Series: A young citizen's
   guide to news literacy | Includes index.
Identifiers: LCCN 2018015450| ISBN 9781538344989 (library bound) | ISBN
   9781538346082 (pbk.) | ISBN 9781538346099 (6 pack)
Subjects: LCSH: Media literacy–Juvenile literature. | Fake news–Juvenile
   literature.
Classification: LCC P96.M4 C57 2018 | DDC 302.23–dc23
LC record available at https://lccn.loc.gov/2018015450

Manufactured in the United States of America

CPSIA Compliance Information: Batch #CWPK19: For Further Information contact Rosen Publishing, New York, New York at 1-800-237-9932

# CONTENTS

# SIFTING THROUGH THE NOISE

From the moment you wake up, you're surrounded with information. Whether it's a push notification on your smartphone or a breaking-news alert on television, there's no escaping the media outlets competing for your attention. All the noise can make it hard to know where to go or what to trust for information.

This information overload has made it easier for misinformation to bubble up to the surface and spread. It can be very confusing. Is an article you read on your smartphone more **credible** than a bit of information your friend tells you? Why are there so many different ways people can tell a single story? In the end, there's still one objective truth. People interested in the news have ways to find it.

## BREAKING NEWS

Twenty-two years ago, 12 percent of adults in the United States read their news online. By 2016, that number had reached 81 percent.

The digital era has made information more abundant than ever, which has made it harder for people to know where to go or whom to trust for their news.

# THE ROLE OF JOURNALISM

The First Amendment of the U.S. Constitution states that, "Congress shall make no law respecting an establishment of religion, or prohibiting [forbidding] the free exercise thereof; or abridging [taking away] the freedom of speech, or of the press; or the right of the people peaceably to assemble, and to petition [ask] the government for a redress [relief from] of grievances [complaints]."

The Founding Fathers felt so strongly about free speech and other freedoms that this amendment became the first one in the Bill of Rights. They felt that a free press was the basis of a free society and the backbone of **democracy**.

People desire information and want the news of the day brought to them in an easy-to-understand way. Fact-based reporting and **journalism** help deliver it.

The First Amendment of the U.S. Constitution protects freedom of speech and says the government can't block or interfere with the sharing of news.

## HOW JOURNALISM MAKES A DIFFERENCE

*Chicago Evening Post* journalist Finley Peter Dunne penned a famous quote about journalism in 1893. Today, it's often remembered as "the job of the newspaper is to comfort the **afflicted** and afflict the comfortable."

That's a basic principle of journalism. A reporter's job is to seek out the truth and share it with the masses, especially when it's for the benefit of the greater good, regardless of how it affects the powerful.

# MEDIA LITERACY: IT'S ON ME

Journalist Brian Stelter once said on his Sunday morning CNN show, *Reliable Sources*, that democracy demands media literacy.

"A lot of well-meaning people don't understand our work," he said on his show in February 2017. "They don't understand who or what to believe."

"Literacy" usually means the ability to read and write. "Media literacy" is often used today to mean the ability to read, understand, and evaluate—or carefully judge the value of—the many types of media we see every day. People who are media literate can identify different kinds of media and understand their messages.

Someone created every bit of media you see or hear for a reason. It's important to identify and understand those reasons, especially since it's easier than ever before to create and share media.

Host of *Reliable Sources* and senior media correspondent Brian Stelter of CNN speaks in 2016 at the American Magazine Media Conference in New York City.

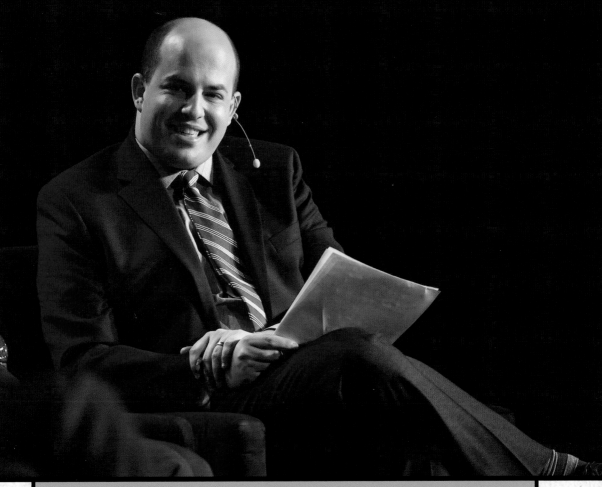

# THE MODERN MEANING OF "FAKE NEWS"

Issues of media literacy recently came to the forefront on the heels of a **turbulent** election cycle that ended with Donald J. Trump winning the presidency. The term "fake news" became popular at that time to describe the spreading of purposely misleading information throughout a busy election cycle. However, the Trump administration later adopted the term and often used it to describe news.

# WHAT'S A CONSPIRACY?

Developing a better understanding of how journalists do their jobs is a good defense against conspiracy theories—especially in the digital information era. But what exactly is a conspiracy theory?

A conspiracy is the act of secretly planning to do something illegal or harmful, or the secret plan itself. A conspiracy theory, therefore, is a theory that uses a conspiracy to explain an event or situation. These theories are often driven by fear and **paranoia** and can damage people's views of the truth.

"Man never landed on the moon." "Elvis Presley is still alive." The most common conspiracy theories used to be so weird that few people would expect them to be true. But as the types of media grow and change, conspiracy theories have become more widespread.

Some people believe that U.S. astronauts never landed on the moon. This conspiracy theory has no basis in fact.

# HEADS IN THE SAND

Sometimes, when someone doesn't want to know the truth, people say they've "got their head in the sand." Fake news feeds into this. It aims to back up what people believe by peddling false information and passing it off as true.

Fake news and conspiracy theories have some things in common. Both of these types of false stories **capitalize** on peoples' beliefs and fears to promote a specific agenda, or plan. Fake news relies on mostly made-up information, while conspiracy theories take a little bit of fact and **embellish** lies around it to create a specific story.

There are ways to combat these fake stories. Understanding the makeup and background of a **legitimate** news story is a great step in the right direction.

## BREAKING NEWS

A study released in 2018 found that fake news stories spread through social media much more quickly than legitimate and factual information.

A regular consumer of fake news is often someone who wants to read only things that match up with their personal beliefs. In other words, they've got their head in the sand to avoid reality.

# WHO WRITES HISTORY?

Fake news and conspiracy theories have been around as long as the written word. The only things that have changed are the ways in which they spread and affect society.

Back in 16th-century Europe, some people thought leaked government reports contained credible information—but others caught on and started leaking fake reports of their own. Those looking for real news had to be very careful and question everything. As printed reports became more widespread, so did their use by people who wanted to spread fake stories about events and other people. Readers had to learn to look for sources and facts.

As long as credible information is published by credible news sources, copycats with fake news will follow. Many still try to take advantage of new kinds of media.

Johannes Gutenberg invented the printing press in 1439, giving birth to a new era of the written word—and also to a new era of spreading false or misleading information.

# REFLECTING FEARS

Fake stories often reflect the fears of people in the time period in which the stories are published. For example, some of the more frequently shared fake stories just after the Civil War revolved around fear of the recently freed African Americans. False reports told of crimes supposedly committed by former slaves. Sometimes these stories led to great violence against black people. Fake stories have also targeted Jewish people throughout history.

# PURPOSE OF FAKE NEWS

If you can understand the reasons someone might want to mislead you with false information, you may be able to identify it more easily. That's why it's so important to understand who gets something from fake news and why.

Many fake stories play to the emotions of a certain group of people and aim to make them angry or upset so they'll do what the creator of the story wants. Often, they try to make people believe something bad about someone else. During election cycles, creators of some stories may seek to convince people to vote for one candidate or another.

It can be tough to tell fake news from real news—especially when the real news seems unbelievable or makes you angry, too! Checking sources is important.

A Dartmouth College study found that 27.4 percent of Americans 18 or older visited a pro-Donald Trump or pro-Hillary Clinton fake news website during the final weeks of the 2016 U.S. presidential campaign.

## WHAT IS SATIRE?

Sometimes a fake story isn't trying to get you to do anything other than read it and maybe laugh at it. Some websites publish satire, which is humor that pokes fun at human foolishness or wrongdoing. It sometimes seeks to improve society by making people think. Satire is a very old form of humor! You may have heard of the website The Onion. This is a satire website. Sometimes, people mistake satire for real news.

# FAKE STORIES, REAL CONSEQUENCES

Fake news and conspiracy theories might seem funny, but they can have serious consequences. In December 2016, a man who'd read a conspiracy theory claiming the Comet Ping Pong restaurant in Washington, D.C., was holding children captive went there to investigate. He took several guns and fired three shots into the restaurant, intending to rescue the fictional children. A number of real news outlets had debunked, or disproven, the conspiracy theory before the incident.

Fake news and conspiracy theories can hurt our world in many other ways. Even leaders and politicians have quoted statistics, or numbers, from bad sources. If this bad information is used to make public policy, it could harm many people. Fake news can also make people distrust real news they should know.

## BREAKING NEWS

Sometimes people write fake news not to fool people or convince them to do something, but just for money. These writers may sell ads on the websites where they post their fake stories.

A person posts a sign outside the Comet Ping Pong restaurant in Washington, D.C., just days after the shooting incident. Fortunately, no one was hurt.

# SOCIAL MEDIA SHOWDOWN

The rise of social media and its great effect on people have helped fake news and conspiracy theories spread. It's very easy to share articles and stories on social media sites such as Facebook and Twitter. Many times, people share these without checking the sources. A link to a bad source may not look so different from a link to a credible source. Readers get confused.

People may not even care if a story is credible as long as it backs up ideas they already have. Many readers tend to look for information that confirms, or proves, their beliefs—and to believe that information backs them up even when it doesn't. This is called confirmation **bias**. People tend to believe what they want to believe.

## BREAKING NEWS

A "bot" is an application that performs an automated task. Bots can be used to power fake social media accounts to spread false or misleading messages online.

One criticism of social media sites is that they tend to show people only the posts that back up beliefs they already have.

## FACEBOOK UPROAR

In early 2018, news broke that a Facebook quiz app had harvested data from millions of Facebook accounts. The app's creator gave this information to a company named Cambridge Analytica. According to reports, that company then used it to influence people's choices in elections, including the 2016 election of Donald Trump. One of the ways it **allegedly** did this was to target them with specific pro-Trump ads and news.

# WHAT TO LOOK FOR

Trying to figure out what news reports to trust can feel overwhelming. One of the first things to do is look at what news source is reporting the story. Credible news outlets often have common features you can look for. A byline with the author's name is a good sign. This also means you can look up the author and find out more about them—and if they even exist! Also, the more established the news source, the more reliable it tends to be.

Double-check the address of the website. Does it lead to an official website? If a site ends with ".co" it may be fake. Look for an actual address for the company's physical site. Check for any signs that the site may publish satire or "fantasy news."

## BREAKING NEWS

The best and most credible news reports are open about where the information comes from. What's the source's background? What's their motive? How do they know the information they shared?

The *Guardian* newspaper app is seen on a smartphone. The *Guardian*, a British newspaper, is a credible news source.

# WHAT ABOUT BIAS?

With the explosion of the digital era, consuming a healthy news diet has become a lot like consuming a healthy food diet. You have many different options to choose from. Some are good for you, and some are bad for you. Too much of the bad stuff can make you sick. And everyone has their own tastes and preferences.

Even reputable news sources can have bias. Always check for sources that stick to the facts. Remember that just because you don't agree with something, that doesn't mean it's biased. Also, check to see if more than one news outlet is reporting the story. One source might break the story, or report it first, but other outlets will soon pick up a good story.

## BREAKING NEWS

The website AllSides.com provides a place for people to rate news outlets based on what they believe about their bias. The Associated Press, Reuters, National Public Radio, and *USA Today* are among the sources people believed to be least biased.

Just like with food, news consumers have different choices for their news diet. It's important to be mindful of a balanced news diet.

# A MATTER OF TRUST

A 2017 study by the Reuters Institute looked into the public's trust of its news organizations across 36 countries. The study found that Finland scored highest in terms of public trust in the news. Greece and South Korea scored the lowest. The study also found a strong connection between distrust of the media and **perceived** political bias, specifically in countries with the greatest political divisions, such the United States, Italy, and Hungary.

# RED FLAGS

Readers must be especially careful while reading information online, in part because anyone can post anything on the Internet. Check stories to see if the news source backs up its claims. Generally, the more unusual the claim, the more evidence the site should provide to support it.

Did you find the story through a social media feed, or is it marked "promoted"? Does it have a headline that doesn't quite match the rest of the story? If you answered "yes" to these questions, that's a red flag. Is there a byline? Does the website have an informative "About" section and an email address that matches the website address? Is there a date on the story? If you answered "no" to any of these questions, that could be a red flag, too.

Traditional newspaper articles have to go through certain steps before they're published. Online sources without a connection to traditional media may not go through these steps.

# STRIKING A MATCH ON SOCIAL MEDIA

In January 2018, a number of fake Twitter accounts claimed to belong to a lottery winner. The owners of these fake accounts claimed they'd share the money with those who shared the post immediately. The post spread like wildfire and became a shining example of just how quickly false information can spread on the Internet. Within a few days, one of the accounts had more followers than the account that really belonged to the lottery winner.

# HELD ACCOUNTABLE

Real news outlets are still run by people, and people aren't perfect. So they, too, are bound to make mistakes. Sometimes, other people use those mistakes to claim media bias or fake news. However, real news outlets hold themselves **accountable** to their readers, viewers, and listeners for errors. By understanding news corrections, news consumers can make better judgments about news sources.

News sources should have their corrections policies posted clearly on their website. A representative of the Poynter Institute, a journalism school, says good policies have three elements, including information on the source's approach to **accuracy**, how it will handle requests for correction, and how it delivers corrections. A news company's efforts to correct errors are, in fact, more evidence of its credibility than if it were unwilling to do so.

According to Poynter, if a news outlet must make a correction on a story that was both online and in print, corrections should run in both types of media.

# KEEP IT REAL

Fake news and conspiracy theories aren't going away, but there are ways we can fight back and avoid those who want to trick us.

By becoming more familiar with real journalism and understanding what goes into news reporting, we can better understand where to find good information and who to trust. We can also learn to avoid fake news stories by finding out more about the tricks they use.

There's good news, too. As more people talk about fake news and its consequences, more people are learning about the problem and coming up with possible solutions. Do you have any ideas? Maybe you can help! You can also help by telling friends and family members what you've learned.

# GLOSSARY

**accountable:** Required to be responsible for something.

**accuracy:** The quality or state of being free of mistakes.

**afflict:** To trouble.

**alleged:** Asserted to be true or exist.

**bias:** A tendency to believe that some people or ideas are better than others.

**capitalize:** To use something in a way that helps you.

**credible:** Reliable, believable.

**democracy:** A government elected by the people, directly or indirectly.

**embellish:** To make something more attractive by adding details or features.

**journalism:** The collecting, writing, and editing of news stories for newspapers, magazines, websites, television, or radio.

**legitimate:** Real or accepted.

**paranoia:** An unreasonable feeling that people dislike you or are trying to hurt you.

**perceive:** To regard as being something.

**turbulent:** Full of confusion and disorder.

# INDEX

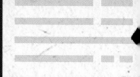

# WEBSITES

Due to the changing nature of Internet links, PowerKids Press has developed an online list of websites related to the subject of this book. This site is updated regularly. Please use this link to access the list: www.powerkidslinks.com/newslit/conspiracy